95

W9-BED-900

3 1192 00567 4195

BALLS
AND
BALLOONS

Ed Catherall

Wayland

Science is Fun

Balls and Balloons	**Growing Plants**
Clay Play	**Light and Dark**
Colours	**Mirrors and Lenses**
Floating and Sinking	**Our Pets**
Fun with Magnets	**Sand Play**
Fun with Wheels	**Wind Play**

Illustrations by George Fryer

First published in 1985 by
Wayland (Publishers) Ltd
61 Western Road, Hove
East Sussex BN3 1JD, England

British Library Cataloguing in Publication Data
Catherall, Ed
Balls and balloons. – (Science is Fun)
1. Flight – Experiments – Juvenile literature
I. Title   II. Series
531'.11'0724   TL547

ISBN 0–85078–600–2

Phototypeset by
Kalligraphics Ltd, Redhill, Surrey
Printed in Italy by
G. Canale & C.S.p.A., Turin
Bound in the U.K. by
The Bath Press, Avon

CONTENTS

Throwing a ball

Go outside and throw a ball.
Watch how the ball moves through the air.
Notice how it is pulled down to the ground.
How far can you throw a ball?

Place a can on the ground.
Throw a ball at the can.
How often can you hit the can in ten tries?

Kicking a ball

Go outside and kick a ball to a friend.
Kick the ball to each other.
Only stop the ball with your legs.
Can you kick a ball further than you can throw it?

Place a can on the ground.
Kick the ball at the can.
Is it easier to hit the can by
throwing or kicking the ball?

Catching a ball

Throw a ball into the air and catch it.
Throw the ball higher and catch it.
What do you notice?

Keep throwing the ball higher and higher.
What can you feel as the ball falls into your hands?

Which of your friends can throw the ball
the highest and still catch it?

Rolling along a line

Use chalk to draw a thick,
straight line on level ground.
On a calm day roll a ball along the line.
How far along the line can you roll the ball?

Try using different balls.
Which ball is the easiest to roll along the line?

Rolling through arches

Cut arches along one side of a sheet of cardboard.
Make the arches different sizes.
Use books to hold your arches upright.
Stand five paces from the arches.

Try to roll a ball through each arch.
Which arch is the easiest
to roll balls through?

Bouncing balls

Make a solid ball from a lump of clay.
Drop your clay ball on flat, hard ground.
Does your clay ball bounce?
What happens to the ball?

Drop a rubber ball on flat ground.
Does your rubber ball bounce?

Try different balls.
Which ball bounces the best?

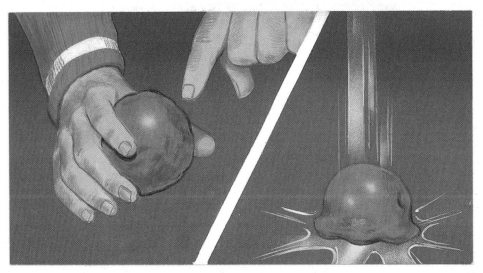

Measuring bounces

Pin a large sheet of paper on to a wall.
Ask a friend to drop a ball from a certain height
on to a smooth, hard surface.
Watch carefully.
Mark the height of the bounce on the paper.

Drop the ball from a greater height.
Mark this bounce.
What do you notice?
Try this with different balls.

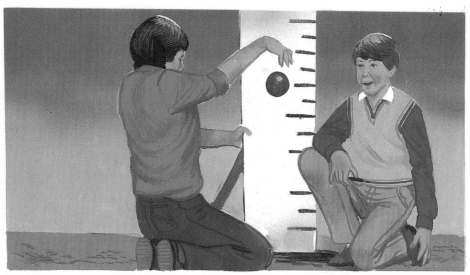

Bouncing on the ground

Drop a rubber ball on hard ground.
How high does the ball bounce?

From the same height, drop the ball on soft ground.
Does the ball bounce as high on soft ground
as it does on hard ground?

Drop the ball from the same height on sand.
Does the ball bounce?
What happens to the sand?

11

The bouncing-ball game

Put a layer of soil or sand into a large bucket.
Place the bucket on flat ground.
Stand back from the bucket.

Try to bounce a rubber ball into
the bucket with one bounce.

How far away from the bucket can you stand and
still bounce the ball into the bucket?
Try this game with your friends.

Bouncing off a wall

Throw a ball against a wall.
Catch the ball as it bounces off the wall.
Notice the path of the ball.

Catch the ball with both hands.
Then try catching the ball with one hand.
Try throwing with different hands.
With which hand do you throw best?

Marbles

Roll a marble so that it bumps another marble.
What happens to each marble?

What happens when one marble hits two marbles?
Which games use balls bumping into each other?

Put three marbles in line.
Make sure that the marbles are touching each other.
What happens when you roll a marble
so that it hits the one at the front of the line?

Balls used in sport

Look at the balls in the picture below.
Which games do the balls represent?

What else is needed to play each game?
What name is given to the playing area?

Notice the size of each ball.
Which balls are hollow and which are solid?
What are the balls made of?
How would each ball bounce?

Rolling down slopes

Find a length of smooth wood.
Place a book on a level floor.
Rest one end of the wood on the book
to make a slope.
Put a ball half way up the slope.
Release the ball and watch it roll down.

How far does the ball roll across the floor?
What happens when you let go of
the ball from higher up the slope?

Inflating a balloon

Ask an adult to inflate a balloon.
Watch the balloon carefully.
What do you see?
Feel the balloon.
What can you feel?

How do you know when the balloon is fully inflated?
What happens if more air is put in to the balloon?

Balloon volleyball

Tie a rope between two sticks.
The rope will act as a net.
Blow up a balloon.

With your hand hit the balloon over
the net to a friend.
Hit the balloon back and forth over the net.
Try to stop the balloon from hitting the ground.

You score one point if the balloon
hits the ground on your friend's side of the net.

18

Jet propelled

Ask an adult to inflate a balloon.
Hold the balloon by the neck, but do not tie it up.
Let go of the balloon.
What happens?
Try this many times.
Does the balloon ever travel neck first?

Notice how your balloon is
propelled like a jet aeroplane.

Balloons that float

Some balloons float in the air.
These balloons are filled with a gas called helium.

Buy a helium-filled balloon.
Take it home.
Release the balloon indoors
and watch it rise to the ceiling.
Tie things to the balloon so that
it just floats in the air.

After several days, what happens to the balloon?

Blowing bubbles

Buy a bubble-blowing kit which has a loop.
Dip the loop into the liquid.
Lift it out.
Is there a skin on the loop?

Shake the loop.
What happens to the skin?

Blow on the skin to make a bubble.
Blow bubbles into the sunlight.
Watch them as they float away.
What do you see?

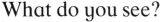

Chasing bubbles

Blow a large soap bubble.
Does the bubble rise as it leaves the loop?
Where does the air in the bubble come from?

Blow on to the back of your hand.
Is this air warm or cold?

Blow bubbles in the wind.
Try to catch the flying bubbles.

Hot air balloons

Ask an adult to inflate a balloon and tie the neck.
Hit the balloon into the air.
Watch it sink.
Measure the balloon.

Ask an adult to heat the balloon with a hair dryer.
Measure the balloon again.
Hit the balloon into the air.
What do you notice?
Have you ever seen hot air balloons?

GLOSSARY

Arch   A curved part that helps support a bridge or building.

Helium   A gas used in balloons and airships which is lighter than air.

Hollow   An object is hollow if it has empty space inside it.

Inflate   To blow something up with air or gas.

Level   Flat and smooth.

Liquid   Something which flows, like water or oil.

Measure   To find out how big something is.

Propel   To make an object move forwards.

Release   To let something go.

Solid   An object is solid if it does not have any empty space inside it.

Volley   To hit or kick a ball before it touches the ground.

INDEX